AF486684

REMINISCENCES OF THE FUTURE

ABHIRAM SARAN

Copyright © Abhiram Saran 2024
All Rights Reserved.

ISBN 979-8-89475-006-4

This book has been published with all efforts taken to make the material error-free after the consent of the author. However, the author and the publisher do not assume and hereby disclaim any liability to any party for any loss, damage, or disruption caused by errors or omissions, whether such errors or omissions result from negligence, accident, or any other cause.

While every effort has been made to avoid any mistake or omission, this publication is being sold on the condition and understanding that neither the author nor the publishers or printers would be liable in any manner to any person by reason of any mistake or omission in this publication or for any action taken or omitted to be taken or advice rendered or accepted on the basis of this work. For any defect in printing or binding the publishers will be liable only to replace the defective copy by another copy of this work then available.

Dedicated in cherished memory to Duke, the most loving German Shepherd a child could ever have.

Contents

KWISATZ HADERACH

I waltzed lazily across a mellow street,

A collection of sunbeams filtering through

The glittering green foliage above me,

My mind contemplating nearly everything

A college student could think about while

Suppressing their desperate cravings for caffeine.

Much to my dismay, my ruminations were broken—

A vibrating cellphone sent ripples through my
jacket,

I flipped my phone around like a delicate balisong,

Cursing the inefficiency of its fingerprint sensors,

I butterfingered past security of my own design,

But my hands went numb when I saw the rejection
email.

In a matter of moments, my vision became blurred,

The unending flow of time came to a grounding halt,

I could see the future unfolding before my eyes,

Yet I was powerless to alter it—I could not move,

My progress across a lifetime rapidly dissolving

In the acidic sands of unbeatable adversity.

I saw myself joining the ranks of billions of men

Who bore the burden of unfulfilled potential,

With self-sabotage blazing through my destiny

Like the red-hot flames of an unquenchable fire,

Yet what agitated me was not the inferno itself,

But the reality that I'd done all I could only to fail.

The voice of reason quelled my visions, as always,

I cannot abdicate my inescapable obsession with affliction,

Yet I know that my prescience simply reflects my mind,

Most of the painful futures I've foreseen haven't materialized,

And the sands of time always seem to wither away

Momentary fears of the horrors of tomorrow.

THE LAST WALK

I'd never really considered how tiring,

A simple stroll across campus could be,

For I'd spent years walking these bustling streets,

Without experiencing the slightest hint of fatigue.

Yet as I trudged solemnly across that ghost town,

I started to realize why I feared this walk so much,

It was my last day at the place that'd been my home,

And I needed the closure of one final goodbye.

As I visited the locations that had defined my
college life,

I watched on in third person as forgotten
memories—

Classes, events, parties, conversations, trauma—

Unfolded in snippets before my quivering eyes.

When I walked by red buildings and friendly classrooms,

I felt that if I squinted my eyes and looked hard enough,

I'd be able to catch a glimpse of my former self inside,

Surrounded by the people that had lit up my life.

I know that I will always have these memories—

Familiarity breeds comfort, after all—

I can always fall into their welcoming arms

When I'm struggling to adapt to the life ahead.

And yet I know that it is only a matter of time

Until they get drowned out in the background,

I'd already forgotten them—they only came back to me

Because I visited the physical locations they occurred in.

As I finished my walk and took one final look at

The setting sun and the campus where I'd rebuilt myself,

I knew I was cursed to remember these final recollections

More vividly than the memories that preceded them.

Separation Anxiety

I can no longer

Ignore the truth

That has been

Staring

At me

Ever since I got my alumni keychain.

Why does something

That should give

Joy

Bring along

As its plus one

A sea of tears?

Home Sick

I cursed the intern who designed this website,

My MacBook's monotonous machinations

Denied me access to the robes I needed,

The timer to graduation ticked relentlessly,

Leaving my fate to Hermes, God of shipping.

The page finally loaded, and I scoffed as I

Judged the naivety of anyone dumb enough

To spend seven latte's worth of cash

In a vain attempt to add to their robe

A tiny seal of their nation's flag.

That triumphant feeling gave way to regret,

When I realized that I had barely hesitated

Before completely discarding the idea of

Carrying a symbol from the land I call(ed) home

With me on the most important day of my life.

I wondered why over winter break I

Never truly felt *at home* at home,

I'd missed the food; I'd missed the sights—

But not even the house I grew up in

Could inspire a sense of belonging in me.

What was the cause of such disconnect?

Was it the trauma, the forgotten memories?

Was it the figures that I couldn't complain about?

Was it the system that had spit me out without care?

Was it the truth that I'd have never really thrived
here?

"Home is where the hearth is",

And yet mine radiates pain, not warmth,

It is quite telling that my worst nightmares

Involve being stranded at "home" with no escape,

Settling for a life of what-could-have-been.

I feel slightly better when I consider

Distance from home might one day

Quell these traitorous thoughts,

Yet each night I go to sleep accepting that

I am destined to live the life of a nomad.

Déjà Vu

I stepped out of the time machine,
And glanced around the dimly lit verandah,
Pausing for a moment to take in sights
That were buried so deep in my memory
I'd forgotten they even existed.

Reminding myself that my visit had a purpose,
I tip-toed my way up the marble staircase,
Making sure to correct my stride as I
Reached that dreaded pair of uneven steps,
I'd tripped on them far too many times before.

I turned left and opened the oak door,
The creaky ceiling-fan masked my footsteps,
Photos and trophies decorated the gray wall,
Enormous textbooks resting on an unused piano,
Memories of a life I'd wiped from my mind.

A sleeping figure disturbed the mess of blankets,

He lay on the pillow I still have to this day,

I knew he was a light sleeper, so I didn't move,

Staring at his face while trying to remember

A time when I had short hair like him.

Does he know? My brain asked me,

Does he know what's about to happen?

What he'll do? What he'll go through?

Does he know what he's going to become?

I clenched my fist and silenced the questions.

I suppressed an ironic smile

As the memories came flooding back,

Thirty seconds in that cozy room

Was all it took to break my resolve,

I ended up aborting the mission and fleeing the scene.

I'd always known time travel was inherently dangerous,

But that lonely night taught me that

The true hazard of messing with time

Wasn't the potential of changing the past,

But the threat of reliving it.

Twin Suns

There is a voice in me that is

Rational

I know it is my own voice

It views my life as a collection of problems

Problems that can be solved given time

It makes sense that this part of me is

Optimistic

It imagines my future self to be

Happy

Successful

Fulfilled

For I've overcome everything I've faced so far

And I should do so in the future as well

And yet there is a voice in me that is

Unreasonable

It is a distorted version of my own voice

It views my life as a collection of pain

Pain that will only grow given time

It makes sense that this part of me is

Terrified

It imagines my future self to be

Panicked

Mediocre

Devastated

For though I've overcome everything I've faced so far

It is only a matter of time until I fail in the worst possible way

I am the planet that orbits this binary star system

Gravitationally bound, unable to escape

There is nothing I can do but wonder

If forces like these can ever reach equilibrium.

❖ ❖ ❖

RABBIT HOLE

I'd often stayed up late at night,

Fiercely burrowing my way through

An endlessly deep Wikipedia rabbit hole.

Looking up literally everything from

Obscure phenomena, to fancy terms,

To history-defining military conflicts.

Those wars always intrigued me,

Millions of lives lost over matters

So trivial you'd never heard of them.

I sometimes wondered how it felt

To watch a war from Wikipedia

Unfold right before my eyes.

Would I be concerned?

Would I be outraged?

Would I be apathetic?

I scoured through dozens of webpages,

None of them could put me in the shoes of

A bystander watching a war in a distant land.

And yet here I lie in a cozy bed,

Watching on as Wikipedia's list of

Ongoing conflicts gains a new entry.

Some curious child will be in

My position thirty years from now,

Accessing a Wikipedia equivalent,

Learning about forgotten battles,

Reading about historical weeks,

That I saw slowly play out.

CEASEFIRE

It's strange.

I almost can't remember a time

When I could look at my future

And see it filled with promise.

Not washed away by the cruel,

Unrelenting waves of uncertainty.

Every time I tried convincing myself

That things would eventually work out,

The frantic part of my brain—it would object,

It would obstruct all rational thought,

Reducing my sessions of reflection to

Flaming messes of unfiltered pessimism.

I've spent so long living this hapless life

That whenever I find a rare moment of peace,

A welcome ceasefire from the battle raging within,

I do not know how to proceed.

I'm not used to hearing utter silence,

From the part of me that is always on edge.

I know that I can probably never win

The exhausting game of chess I play against

The part of me that is obsessed with

Imagining everything I built fall apart,

But my absence from peacetime has taught me

That there are much worse games to play.

TSUNDOKU

I was addicted to reading as a child,

A stack of novels on my bedside table,

My curiosity was satiated through endless tomes,

Every sentence within left an imprint on me.

My identity was shaped by the books I read,

And I embraced the life of a bibliophile,

For I had finally reached a stage where

I wasn't really myself if I wasn't reading.

Yet now, my to-read stack threatens to overflow,

The mind that finished 600-page novels overnight

Struggles hopelessly to string together

But one hour of uninterrupted reading.

My failed attempts at finishing a book,

In truth, desperate yearnings to connect

With the child who used to enjoy such things.

I do not know when I stopped being him.

Perhaps I grew up, perhaps it was burnout,

I do not have the time or effort to read,

But I feel unmistakably comfortable

When I have piles of books around me.

There will come a day when I finally regain my purpose,

A day of peace, tranquility, and utter satisfaction,

Until then, I take solace in the knowledge that

If I can't enjoy reading books, I can cherish collecting them.

EDIFICE

Whenever my peers told me in passing,

The exact location of their ideal vacation,

I felt confused because I didn't have one,

I didn't have a singular dream destination.

Yet the Pyramids have always captured my
attention,

Not for their grandeur or for the sands of the desert,

But because they are the oldest gravestone we have,

The oldest mark of human excellence on this planet.

I hope to one day touch the side of a pyramid,

And run my fingers across the decaying jagged rock

That was carved through hours of unforgiving labor,

The only reminder of a people that once were.

Perhaps when I do that, I will be connecting

With everyone who once thought my thoughts,

And maybe in some unimaginably distant time,

Another being may do the same for me.

Daybreak

I wasn't expecting much from this flight,

A 5 AM takeoff isn't the best for sightseeing,

So as the A320 reached its abode in the skies,

I accepted that the faded red runway lights

Would be the defining memory of my trip,

An acceptable outcome, given my sleep-
deprivation.

As I rested against the cool glass window,

I saw scattered white wisps of smoke-like clouds

Dominate a night sky that slowly became gray,

This gradual color change had me perplexed

Until I remembered that we were flying east,

Right towards the boundary of day and night.

A few minutes later, my eyes met daylight,

The pitch-black sky started to represent

A void invaded by streaks of pastel blue,

I saw storm clouds so close to the ground

That they looked like great mountain ranges,

Blessing the earth with their sacred water.

Beneath them, sparkling dots of artificial light

Gently illuminated a slumbering city,

I looked back to the direction we came from

And saw the cover of darkness retreating,

Ahead of us, the unyielding rays of sunshine

Pierced through the clouds and lit up the city below.

I've always tried to find new additions to

My list of things to look forward to in the future,

It's filled with stuff I'd experience once or twice,

But after that flight over the day-night boundary,

I think I should try to look forward to appreciating

The simple beauty hidden in everyday life.

❖ ❖ ❖

Happy Anniversary!

8:30 PM, March 2nd, 2023:

The fountain's brilliant yellow lights battle

Against the all-encompassing darkness,

I stand still at its foot, Nocturne Op. 9 No. 2

Reverberating through my headphones.

This is the exact day,

This is the exact time,

This is the exact place,

Where I had relapsed two years prior.

I take in a breath, trying to remember

What hitting rock bottom felt like,

Yet all I found in the back of my head,

Was a blur of fear, pain, and utter dread,

My mind had chosen to forget the rest.

I'd questioned the worth of my life

More often than I'd care to admit,

The urge to end it was ever present,

Always waiting for a chance to strike.

And yet I endured, I healed, I learned,

But all it took to wash that growth away,

Was the faintest possibility that I'd messed up,

That I'd ruined my only chance at a good future,

So, my mind decided that I should have no future.

The thought passed like a fleeting shadow,

And I was left with shame and consequence.

I'd thrown away seven months of progress,

Over an idea that barely lasted a second.

I think back to last year's anniversary,

I'd camped at the fountain for a whole hour,

Not a word spoken, not a thought formed,

A jubilee marked by cold, blank stares.

I did not know then

If I came to the fountain

To commemorate a year of peace

Or to visit the memorial

Of the child that once was.

A single tear escapes my right eye,

I gently take off my headphones

And embrace the sounds of night,

The gravity of it all finally hits me.

Every thought where I celebrate

Two whole years since my last relapse,

Is countered by another one carrying

Reminders of the pain I went through,

Forces like these cannot reach equilibrium.

I crossed this fountain every day,

But only truly visited it once annually,

My last encounter left me completely numb,

Leaving me no choice but to return again this year.

But now, everything feels different,

I know I can't come back next year,

And that my next visit to this fountain

Will feature not melancholy and regret,

But degrees, photos, and graduation robes.

My last relapse, in truth, occurred

Because I thought I had no future,

The next time I visit its obituary

I will have secured my future.

I turn away and bid the fountain adieu,

Perhaps I am out of the woods,

Perhaps I have genuinely healed,

Perhaps I have finally made it,

Perhaps my life is worth living.

VALEDICTION

It is difficult not to think that

Every finished chapter

Signifies the closing of a book

When I do not know

How many pages are left.

It is difficult not to worry about

The fate of my story's characters

When I flip the page over

And find a blank white sheet

Staring right back up at me.

And yet it is difficult not to cherish

The sentences of paragraphs gone by,

Compressing four years of life

Into an unfinished sine curve,

Jumbled together in fragments of memory.

I have written hundreds of pieces,

Stories, poems, failed book drafts,

They all arose from an empty canvas,

Like them, my song remains unwritten,

I think it is time for me to write it.

www.ingramcontent.com/pod-product-compliance
Lightning Source LLC
Chambersburg PA
CBHW051419130726
47989CB00007B/2992